Praise for Shelley Stile's
95 Transformational Tips for
Letting Go and Moving On
After Your Divorce

Having practiced primarily in family law for many years, in addition to my work as a judge pro tem and conducting settlement conferences, I found Shelley's tips to be an excellent source of strength. They provide a common sense direction for those going through this difficult time of divorce. Frankly, as a step parent who has had to deal with "our own litigation" issues, these tips were personally helpful to me.

Professionally, I know divorce can be trying and what so many people lack is direction. These tips, having come from someone who has had such a life experience, are extremely meaningful. I plan to provide the book to clients who are going through this process in the hopes that these tools may make the divorce process easier on them.

Ronee Korbin Steiner
ATTORNEY AT LAW
SCOTTSDALE, ARIZONA

95 Transformational Tips for Letting Go and Moving On After Your Divorce, by Shelley Stile offers relevant, tactical thoughts to get you through the divorce transition with peace and self-awareness.

We all need a little help as embark on one of the most difficult periods in our lives and Shelley offers up just that help. *95 Transformational Tips for Letting Go and Moving On After Your Divorce* is a quick, easy to read guide that will make a great impact!

Michelle Muncy,
PRESIDENT—CHILDSHARING.
COM/ ONLINE
CO-PARENTING PROGRAM.

Shelley's book has been very helpful to me as a woman separated from her husband. I found the advice both practical and deeply "spiritual" and I particularly liked the uplifting "coach approach" emphasizing self awareness and empowerment, choice, and the encouragement to see gift and opportunity in the situation. If it is helpful to me as a separated woman, I can only imagine how helpful it would be to someone who is divorced, or going through the process.

Katherine L. Poehnert,
M.ED.PSYCH., PCC
INSIGHT

95 Transformational Tips for Letting Go and Moving On After Your Divorce by Shelley Stile should be required reading for all people going through a divorce or separation. When you are feeling alone and hurt, wondering how you will ever survive your life after divorce, just start reading the words of wisdom found in this gem of a book.

It's like sitting on the front porch with a sage old friend who has seen and done it all, and who is willing to share the lessons from past experiences. Nuggets about accepting the reality of your situation, letting go of blame, taking responsibility for you new life, and realizing that what your ex is doing is no longer your business are all in there, plus much, much more. What I loved about this book is the bite-sized, easily digestible advice that you can put to work for you right now. You'll want to keep it handy as you rebuild your life and even beyond, because the lessons and wisdom will apply to all parts of your life. As the author says, "Your divorce is not a mistake. It is an opportunity to learn and then go on to create the life you truly want." This book can help you do that.

Tracy Achen
Editor of WomansDivorce.com

Divorce recovery doesn't happen overnight. If readers can process just one tip a day—in three months they will emerge stronger, healthier, and ready to embrace their new life. Shelley's tips are a great reminder of the power of intention and positive thinking. I highly recommend reading and re-reading this book to help focus your attention in the right direction.

Noah B. Rosenfarb, CPA, ABV, PFS, CDFA
ACCOUNTANT AND FINANCIAL ADVISOR
FOR DIVORCING WOMEN
WWW.FREEDOMDIVORCEADVISORS.COM

95 *Transformational Tips for*

Letting Go and Moving On

After Your Divorce

SHELLEY STILE

DIVORCE RECOVERY LIFE COACH

www.lifeafteryourdivorce.com

Contents

Introduction

Divorce is a major life transition that shakes the very foundation of our lives. It is an emotional upheaval the likes of which we could never have imagined. Your very identity is in tatters. If you had defined yourself as a wife or husband, that label no longer applies. Who are you now?

Your thoughts and emotions seem out of control and overwhelming. This tornado will ultimately pass, but there are some very specific things that you can do right now so that you are able cope more effectively with both your emotional and legal divorce. You need a focused and rational mindset to handle everything that is to come. Within the 95 Tips, you will find invaluable tools and skills to assist you in navigating this tumultuous landscape.

Once you have weathered the storm of the grieving period that follows the loss of your marriage, you begin the task of letting go of the pain of the past, of being in acceptance of this new reality and moving forward to create a new and hopefully better life after your divorce. Again, there are explicit steps that you can take that will facilitate the recovery process and guide you to access your own inner wisdom.

Through my own personal experience with divorce as well as my years of coaching people, I have found a number of powerful methods that aid in coping, in healing, and in letting go and moving on.

Like any other method of personal growth, change takes commitment and effort on your part. It does not happen overnight. It is not enough to read through these tips. You must commit to making a daily effort to incorporate them into the fabric of your life. Your success in your own healing process is wholly dependent on the effort you expend. What you put in is what you will get out of this process.

Many of these tips were discovered via my own recovery. Others came to light and proved extremely helpful while coaching my clients. Still others are a result of research and reading on

my part. I want to acknowledge the following authors for their
insights and suggest that you read their books:

Janet and Chris Atwood: *The Passion Test*

William Bridges, Transitions: *Making Sense of Life's Changes*

Richard Carson, *Taming Your Gremlin*

Doc Childre & Howard Martin, *The Heartmath Solution*

Debbie Ford, *Spiritual Divorce*

John W. James & Russell Friedman, *The Grief Recovery Handbook*

Dr. Fred Luskin, *Forgive for Good*

Eckhart Tolle, *The Power of Now*

I can assure you that even though it may not seem possible at this
point in time, you will survive this very difficult life transition.
You will learn incredible lessons that you can employ throughout
the rest of your life. You will come to access your own inner
wisdom and to know from your deepest core exactly what needs
to be done in order to create the life that you both want and
deserve. All it takes is your commitment to yourself.

All my best,
Shelley Stile
DIVORCE RECOVERY LIFE COACH
www.lifeafteryourdivorce.com

1

This, too, shall pass.

When you are in pain, you cannot think straight. I promise you that where you are and what you are feeling now is not how you will feel tomorrow, next month, next year, or forever.

You have to feel in order to heal. This phase, immediately after your separation or divorce, is a tremendous challenge.

Just know that things will change and that you will not feel this way forever. Feelings change all the time. They are transient.

Know that you will survive. We all do. Have faith that having survived this huge challenge, you will be a much stronger and wiser person, and that wisdom and strength will allow you to move forward and create a new and vibrant life.

2

Notice the voice in your head—the Gremlin!

*I*s there a voice in your head that is constantly talking and attempting to sabotage your life? Is that little voice, which I refer to as your *gremlin*, telling you that you won't make it on your own, that you'll be alone for the rest of your life, that you are unlovable, that you are stupid, a failure, and doomed?

That's your gremlin speaking. A gremlin, born of the past and your wounded ego, that wants nothing better than to hold you back and keep you stuck in your pain. Your gremlin is not you.

Just notice it, thank it for sharing, ignore its advice, and let it go. Don't trust that voice, because it does not speak the truth. That gremlin, which by the way has been around for most of your life, speaks with a forked tongue! It lies.

You are not the gremlin in your head; you are the person observing the gremlin! Just noticing it and separating yourself from it is the way to tame your gremlin. Better yet, give it a name that describes who it is to you! My gremlin is Angelika, that little brat from the Rugrats cartoon! By naming your gremlin, you recognize it as a separate being from yourself.

Don't argue with a gremlin because it is not rational. Don't engage it in any way other than noticing it and then choosing to ignore it.

That's the way to tame a gremlin!!

3

Write a speech that will be read at your funeral.

I n order to help define who you want to be, write your eulogy. What do you want people to say about you when you pass on? How do you want to be remembered? Exactly who do you want to be for the rest of your life?

Write a eulogy about yourself as if it is being read by someone you know and love. Have them truly express the legacy you want to leave behind. Go into detail.

Now is the perfect time for you to become the person you have always wanted to be, the person whom you will describe in your eulogy.

Are you presently being everything that you have outlined in your eulogy? If you want to be known as a kind and compassionate person, is that who you are being now?

Write your eulogy, and be that person today.

4

Consider your prevalent mood and attitude.

How would you describe your prevalent mood and attitude toward life these days? How would your friends describe it? Are you always negative? Are you angry? Hopeful? Your attitude or mood is your perspective on life, which either serves you or harms you.

Is your perspective a gift or a price you are paying? Try changing your perspective so that it helps you in your recovery and future. Remember, your attitude not only changes the way you see things, it can also change the way things actually are!

Try dropping the doom and gloom, because if that is how you see things, then that is probably how life will show up for you. Choose an attitude that will be an ally not an enemy.

5

Be fully conscious.

When we are conscious, we are extremely aware of our actions, emotions, and thoughts and how they affect our life. We think before we react or choose. We recognize that there might be emotional baggage behind our actions and thoughts and we don't allow that baggage to run the show. We notice our unconscious motivations and take back control of our life.

Being aware and conscious means being in touch with yourself and recognizing the things that have been running you for years. Being conscious means being cognizant of the clues that our bodies and minds send us when we are going into upset. Being conscious is being aware of that incessant negative mind chatter in our head and consciously choosing not to allow it to sabotage us. Being aware means we notice when we are reacting out of habit versus choice.

Finally, being conscious allows us to make real choices versus reacting on an unconscious level, which is not a choice at all. Unconscious reactions render us powerless to control our lives.

Wake up and be conscious.

6

What has your divorce gifted you?

*I*n every experience in life there is the opportunity for deep learning and new wisdom. If you don't take advantage of the lessons that life is handing you, then the experience is in part wasted.

If you went through a painful divorce, what did you learn about what a good relationship might look like? How would you be in a relationship the next time around that is different from before? What did you learn about yourself that you could take forward with you? How have you grown? What hidden strengths have you uncovered? What have you learned about family and friends? What new possibilities have you discovered for yourself? Where do opportunities exist for you now?

There are many gifts that you will come to discover from your divorce. Every single day, there are new opportunities in which you can learn and grow as a human being. There are things that you can do now that you couldn't have done before. There are gifts to be had.

7

Try doing it differently.

Albert Einstein was quoted as saying, "The definition of insanity is doing the same thing over and over again and expecting different results"!

This advice is applicable in every situation in life. You aren't getting along with your ex? Try a different approach. Like any good scientist, it's just a matter of trial and error, learning what doesn't and does work.

Doing the same thing over and over again is a habit, and habits can be broken. Start today.

8
Change habitual behavior.

Most of our behaviors are learned early in life and become habitual. Therefore, it only stands to reason that we can learn new behaviors and create new habits. Science has proven that indeed we can do just that!

A new habit can be created and cemented into the grooves of your brain if you adhere to that new behavior for a minimum of three months. So if you find that you have the habit of speaking before you think, work on changing it by consciously committing to stopping and thinking before you speak.

The human brain is a remarkable instrument, very pliable and capable of learning new ways of being with simple but consistent repetition. You are not doomed to repeat mistakes. The neural groves in your brain that have been set down over the years can be replaced with new grooves by your own conscious volition.

Repave your brain.

9

Put all your attention on your intention, and forget the other stuff.

S ay you intend to let go of the pain of your divorce. That's your stated intention. Now commit to putting all your attention toward fulfilling that goal.

What you do every day should be aligned with that intention; drop anything that distracts you from your goal. Be like someone training for a marathon: Keep your eye on the goal, and do everything in your power to attain it while not allowing anything else to get in the way of your pursuit.

10
Pay attention to your body's messages.

Your body speaks to you all the time, but you probably aren't listening. Do you often realize after it is too late that your back is totally out of whack, your neck is in spasms, or your stomach is in knots? It didn't happen overnight.

The stresses of life leave their mark on our physical self, in tension, muscle pain, headaches, etc. If we are more conscious of our bodies on a daily basis, we will notice the cues they are begging us to hear. We can then act upon those cues and keep ourselves in a state of equilibrium, which will make life easier and more enjoyable.

During and after a divorce, you need all the self-care and nurturing attention you can get! Listen to your body.

11

Find a way to quiet yourself.

Combat stress, anxiety, and anger with a calming practice such as yoga or meditation. Sometimes all it takes is three minutes of deep breathing to calm ourselves so that we can operate on an even keel, think clearly, and make rational decisions and choices.

Our heart rate is responsible for setting the rhythm of our entire body, so making certain your heart rate is slow and even will create calm in both your body and your mind. The heart actually sends electrical impulses to your brain and vice versa. It's all connected.

Whether it is deep breathing with a visualization of something joyful in your life, a walk in nature, yoga, meditation, or whatever works for you, allow yourself time every single day to combat the debilitating effects of stress.

Your ability to handle your divorce will improve dramatically.

12

Learn to accept reality as it is and not as you think it should be.

Acceptance is the most important step in divorce recovery. It is imperative that you consciously acknowledge reality for what it is and exactly as it exists. Once you have done that, you need to move into the full acceptance of what is versus what you think should be.

Should-be and could-be and I-want-it-to-be are fantasyland; a totally subjective viewpoint that has nothing to do with what your life actually is today. Should-be is also a clear sign that you have not yet accepted your divorce and are resisting reality. It's akin to not wanting to believe that your child is sick. If you resist the fact of the illness, then you cannot do anything to help your child. You wouldn't do that to your child, so why do it to yourself?

Should-be keeps you stuck in the pain and in the past. When you accept life for what it is, you can then move forward to make powerful choices and decisions on how you plan to live it in the future.

13

Practice letting go of things that don't serve you, such as your marriage!

We hold on to many things associated with our divorce that cause us heartache and do us harm. Anger, bitterness, and resentment are all emotions that hurt us and us alone and not our ex.

If you have 24 hours in a day to be alive, why would you choose to spend it in self-imposed misery? Choose instead to let go of the things that do not serve you.

Consider the price you pay for negative emotions, and ask yourself: Is it worth it? I doubt it. Remember, you have one life to live. Don't waste any more of your time in hurt.

14

What will you do with this one precious life?

*U*nless you know something that I don't, you have but one precious life to live and that life is short. How will you spend your time? You get to choose. Will you look for the new opportunities as a result of this divorce experience? Will you let go of the pain and embrace change? Who will you be in your future?

What would you regret never having done in your life? Think about that question because it can prove to be the blueprint for your time on earth. Would you regret never having forgiven your ex? Would you regret never having traveled to Europe? Would you regret never having learned how to swim?

Remind yourself every single day that this is it: Your one time around. Don't squander your life in sorrow, bitterness, or pain. It's a waste of your life.

15
Trust yourself.

*T*rust yourself. Do you second-guess your every move? Do you look to others to make the major decisions that will affect your life? If someone questions your choices, do you immediately question them as well? Do you then submit to their will?

Consider that you know yourself better than anyone else and therefore you probably know what's best for you. Even if you didn't in the past, you sure do now!

Try going with what your gut tells you, your intuition.

Certainly listen to what others might offer, BUT make the final decision yourself.

Scientific research tells us that our emotional and mental experiences are stored within our brain and when we go to make a decision, if we access our intuition, it will give us a much more accurate decision then just our brain.

Listen closely to what your heart tells you instead of your head. You can think any situation to death, but your heart or your core wisdom usually has the right answer.

16
Get support.

Who said you had to go it alone? Getting support in any area of your life is a wonderful way to feel nurtured and supported, and, hey, you just might get some answers to your questions.

Ultimately, your life is up to you and in your control only, but support from others is truly beneficial, especially in trying times, and divorce is a trying time to say the least!

We get by with a little help from our friends! Whether it is a friend, a support group, a coach, a therapist, or a clergyperson, avail yourself of some support.

17
Champion yourself!

Way to go! You done good today! You probably spend a good deal of time berating and beating yourself up these days, but when was the last time you championed yourself?

I have a dear friend who has beaten cancer twice, and she pooh-poohs that accomplishment! Can you imagine? I remind her that if she has the strength and courage to face down cancer, she can do anything. It just goes to show how little we acknowledge all that we do right.

It doesn't have to be a fight with cancer. Look at your life, and notice the times that you were successful and the times that you effectively handled adversity. Give yourself a big pat on the back and congratulate yourself for all that you do manage and accomplish.

Going through a divorce is one of the toughest things that you will ever do, so acknowledge how much you are handling these days and give yourself a big thank-you.

Don't wait for someone else to champion you—Do it yourself! You deserve it.

18
There are no mistakes.

Mistakes are just rehearsals for your end goal. They are mis-takes. They show you how not to do something. They are incredible opportunities for important learning and forward movement if you recognize them as life lessons.

Thomas Edison spent years working on the electric light bulb. Each time he didn't get it right, he labeled that an accomplishment because he knew what not to do on the road to what would work. He looked at a mistake through a positive lens.

Your divorce is not a mistake. It is an opportunity to learn and then to go on to create the life you truly want.

19

Life is chaotic—period.

H ere's what you need to get: Life is chaotic. It's wild and crazy, and there is always something unexpected popping up just when you think you are almost free and clear. That's life.

Know that the nature of the universe, which includes you, is chaotic, and don't expect it to be any different. Life is in a continual state of change. Accept that fact, and chaos will not disturb you as much.

20
Fear and doubt are signs of our personal expansion.

*E*veryone experiences fear and doubt when they are about to embark on something new—like life after divorce. It's a normal reaction. It's the fear of the unknown.

Recognize that fear and doubt will appear when you are about to stretch yourself, take a risk, attempt to change, in other words when you are about to move forward in your life.

Recognize that fear, and use its energy to move forward. Have faith in yourself and your future instead of being fearful.

Facing your fears and doubts with forward action is pure empowerment.

21

Consider what worked for you in the past.

When you are stuck or overwhelmed, think about what worked for you in challenging situations in the past. Examine your past accomplishments to see if you can identify what helped you to get things done or to overcome hardships.

How did you do it last time? Be specific. Understand that if in your past you have managed to overcome obstacles, fix problems, and take on challenges, then you can do it again.

22
Don't add meaning where there is none.

*I*f you can master this, you are on your way to a new life. What we do to ourselves! We add meaning where there is none, and then we feel miserable. Classic example: Your ex had an affair. You decide that this affair means you are undesirable, unlovable, and a failure—Get it?

Who knows the real reason they cheated. Maybe it's just in their DNA or some unresolved issue from the past, but it doesn't have to mean something negative about you. You have to recognize that it is you and only you who have chosen the meaning attached to the affair. You create the misery for yourself.

The fact is that person had an affair, and the meaning you create is that you are unlovable. That meaning is not factual. Start separating the facts from the meanings. The "meanings" are making you feel terrible, maybe more so than the affair itself!

23

Accept all of you— the good and the so-called bad.

We are a package deal: with our good points and not so good points; our eccentricities and quirks; our strengths and our weaknesses.

No one is perfect—We leave that to the higher power. Just concentrate on your good points, and accept everything about yourself. Even better, consider that what you call a bad point might come in handy in certain situations.

For instance, you might feel that you are bossy and have deemed that bad. However, I'll bet that there are many situations where being "bossy" will come to work to your advantage.

Accepting everything about yourself is not condoning bad behavior or not trying to learn and grow. Acceptance means you understand that you have all the characteristics that exist in the world and that you are a mirror of the universe. With understanding, you can then choose how to control the characteristics that need controlling.

24
Are you really making choices?

Do you choose of your own free will, or are your choices simply knee-jerk reactions?

As human beings we are gifted with free will, which means that we get to consciously choose what is in our best interest. Choice involves thought and consideration. What we choose will impact our lives. Something as simple as what we eat for breakfast, or as complex as the legal agreement for our divorce, all demand our free will, not our emotional reactions.

Stop and think carefully before you choose. Don't let your emotions dictate your future.

25

Understand the total futility of worrying about what you cannot control or predict.

Think about it: We only worry about what might happen, aka the future, whether it's a minute away or a year away. Given the fact that we have no control over the future and cannot even begin to predict what tomorrow holds, exactly what do we accomplish through worry? We cause ourselves sleepless nights, fear, heartache, and anxiety,not to mention the waste of precious time and energy.

If you have to worry, try worrying about something you can do something about, and then do it. Also try this motto: I'll cross that bridge when I get to it.

26

Who are you? Not your roles or labels, but who are you at your core?

Take away your roles and labels—mother, father, daughter, son, cousin, doctor—Strip those things away, and then ask yourself: "Who am I?"

You may find that you don't have an answer, and if that is the case, start thinking about who you really are and who you want to be. Be more than a label: Be you!

You are a totally unique human being who will never be replicated again in the history of this universe. It is time to reconnect with who you really are, at your core, your passions, and your values—the true you.

27

Life is constant change, so go with the direction of your life's flow.

Nothing in this universe is static, especially us. Everything and everyone is in a constant state of change, and to fight change is not only futile but crazy!

Go with the direction of the flow of your life. Don't resist it, because what you resist, persists! Understand that change is growth, forward movement, and progress. Even when change is unexpected and painful, there is always opportunity hidden inside. Use change as an opportunity, do not see it as a punishment.

Imagine the flow of a fast-moving river. Now consider what it feels like to swim against the current of that river or to go with the flow of it. In flowing with your life's direction, you will have the power to make choices that will lead you to a new and vibrant life.

28

"Tell the truth, the whole truth, and nothing but the truth!"

*I*f I had to choose the most powerful tool for personal transformation and ultimate happiness, it would have to be honoring the truth. Setting aside ego and fear and facing the truth allows you to make powerful and lasting changes and choices in life.

You cannot fool yourself for that long, and if you do you'll pay a big price. Denial leaves you totally powerless to change. Drop your interpretations, your story, and your drama, and look the truth in the eye.

Imagine if you went to a doctor looking for a cure to an illness but you did not tell her all your symptoms. How could she make a diagnosis and help you?

"The truth will set you free."

29
Discover your purpose, and go for it!

We are all here for a reason. To discover the why of our existence is unbelievably powerful. It could be raising two responsible children. It could be to contribute to the needy or to be an advocate for abused women. It could be to run a Fortune 500 company that provides employment to thousands. The list is endless.

My divorce gifted me with a special knowledge, and now my purpose in life is to empower people after divorce.

You are a totally unique individual who has a purpose, which can be found by looking at your passions, your strengths, your special knowledge gleaned from experience, and your desire to leave behind a legacy. Once you find that purpose, your life takes on a new dimension that adds tremendous meaning and joy to your life.

Find your purpose.

30
Practice gratitude.

*O*ne of the keys to happiness is the act of gratitude.

Research clearly demonstrated that people who kept gratitude journals reaped many positive benefits: They exercised more regularly, felt better about their lives, were more energetic, more accepting, and more optimistic—just to name a few of the rewards of being grateful.

Gratitude is especially important during the turmoil of a divorce, when our perspective can become so negative.

Think of what you do have and not what you don't have. Find your blessings and your gifts. Accentuate what is right versus what is wrong.

It will work miracles in your life.

31
Stay away from comparison!

Comparing yourself to someone else usually sets you up for disappointment and regret. There is always someone with seemingly more money, a more exciting career, a bigger house, and better health.

The truth is you don't really know the true quality of other people's lives. No one knows what goes on behind closed doors: Your neighbor's seemingly perfect marriage is probably far from it!

If you need to compare, try doing it with someone less fortunate.

32

The test of your true character will come forth in the tough times, not the good ones.

*T*he tough times in our lives clearly reveal what we are made of. It's easy to be happy when everything is going your way. It's the tough times that truly define us.

Faced with the challenge of divorce, we can discover strength we never knew we possessed. Not only that, but these tough times always have hidden gifts for us, life lessons that empower us.

33

It's not what happens in life, it's how you handle it!

*L*ife is always going to throw us curveballs, and divorce is one of the biggest curveballs we will ever face, second only to the death of a loved one in terms of loss.

If we accept that life will always present us with fresh challenges, we won't be as upset when they appear. Recognizing the fact that life is continually handing us obstacles to overcome, we can then be more accepting and less likely to be angry or resentful.

It's not what life throws our way that determines the quality of our lives, but rather how we choose to handle what life throws our way.

34
Prioritize!

*P*rioritize your to-do list. On a daily or weekly basis, decide what is truly important in the grand scheme of things-to-do, and put those on the top of your list.

Let the other stuff slide for a while. If you think that there are too many things that MUST get handled, I submit to you that you aren't really prioritizing. It might not be a necessity to get to the cleaners today. It would be nice but not a disaster if it didn't happen.

Do the same in your life. Decide what truly matters to you, and make certain those things show up in your life on a daily basis. If you value time with your family, make the time now.

35

Everything works out—Just don't expect it all to work out in a particular way!

*E*verything works out in life though not necessarily the way you wanted or envisioned it all to work out. Nonetheless, it works out.

You may have thought your marriage would last forever, but it didn't. It was never your intention to have it end. You didn't get married in order to get divorced. You did the best you could with the resources you had at hand at the time.

Life takes all sorts of twists and turns. We get challenged. We overcome. We are happy and sad. Things work out one way or another—Just don't expect them to work out to your particular liking all the time.

36
Practice patience.

*L*ife simply doesn't always adhere to your schedule or desires. Patience is a gift and a skill you give to yourself.

Patience takes practice. Like any other habit, it takes time to establish it. Start practicing patience now. Look for disciplines, such as meditation, that will increase your patience.

Consider the costs of impatience: upset, stress, confrontation, and frustration. Is it worth it? Again I ask what price do you pay for impatience? Sitting in a traffic jam can either be a frustrating and exhausting experience or a chance to learn to just let go.

What gifts would be available to you if you learned a little more patience with life? Less stress? Peace of mind? Better health? Better relationships?

The fact is that we don't have the kind of control over life that would allow everything to go according to our timetable or desires. Do yourself a big favor and learn a little patience.

37
What do you fear?

Your fears are the things that hold you back from taking the necessary steps toward a new life after divorce, so exactly what are you afraid of? Of being alone forever? Of not being able to handle it all? Of suffering forever? Of the unknown? Examine yourself, and determine what you fear.

Recognize your fears and understand that they are based in what you cannot be certain of or control. They are like other feelings in that they come and go and change all the time. Doing what you fear the most is incredibly empowering and grants you tremendous momentum.

Remember what it was like when you first saw a tall roller coaster? I was scared to death and I wouldn't go on one until my own kids persuaded me, and I loved it! All that fun and excitement at the amusement parks over the years that wasn't enjoyed!

Don't let your fears hold you back or dictate your life.

38
Watch out for self-righteous positions.

Are you being self-righteous about your divorce? Do you keep making your ex wrong and you right? Are you being high and mighty?

Self-righteous positions are a sure sign that you are stuck in your past and that you continue to hold on to blame. Blame makes you a victim, and victims have no power. Self-righteousness is also a sure indicator of you resisting your life.

There is a big difference between self-righteousness and righteousness. One is destructive, and one contributes to the world. They are light years apart.

Notice if you have any self-righteous positions. If you do, be totally honest with yourself and discover the whys behind your positioning. Then consider very carefully the costs to you and your future.

39
Set boundaries with your ex.

*D*uring and after your divorce process when you are emotionally and mentally raw, keep yourself safe by establishing firm boundaries with your ex.

For instance, your home is now your home, not theirs. Establish new procedures. If you get upset when you speak to your former spouse, limit your conversations or don't have them at all. Make certain they know that when a conversation starts heading south, you will terminate the conversation and resume it only when everyone is rational and in a safe place. If need be, let the attorneys handle as much as possible.

Keep yourself at a safe distance from your ex in all aspects of your life until the divorce is over and you have established some emotional equilibrium again.

You need to keep yourself away from any emotional entanglements right now because there is still an emotional cord between the two of you. You want to limit any emotional triggers.

Communicate to your ex firm ground rules. Learn to say no. Take charge of your recovery.

40
Your divorce story needs changing!

We each have a story of our divorce, and for the most part these stories are disempowering, highly negative, and downright depressing. They make us feel bad and turn us into victims. Not only will your friends get tired of hearing this same old sorry story, but you will, too!

Change your story to empower yourself. Go from being a victim to being the hero of your story. You can interpret your story any way you want to, so interpret it to your own benefit and personal growth.

What does your story read like? Is it sad? Does it make you a victim? Is it filled with resentment and anger? Does your divorce story make you feel good or bad?

Go back and rewrite your story so that it is empowering. Tell how you are growing and changing for the better. Tell how much you have accomplished, and all you have learned. Make it a story that serves as a springboard into a new chapter of a life filled with grand possibilities.

You might not be ready to rewrite your story at this exact point in time, but make certain you rewrite it soon.

41
Beware of unenforceable expectations!

At our core we have established beliefs about life that we have long held, some conscious and many more subconscious. Perhaps we expect life to be fair and people to be kind. Sometimes these beliefs are confirmed and sometimes repudiated. That's life.

Unfortunately, many of these core beliefs or expectations are simply unrealistic, i.e. we cannot enforce them because we do not have that kind of control over life. Yet another lesson in some of our futile behavior.

Right now you may be experiencing some of these unenforceable expectations: I expect my ex to be emotionally supportive and to grant me financial security—Both are unrealistic and totally unenforceable.

These expectations lead to disappointment and resentment. We set ourselves up to feel bad.

Acknowledge the true reality of the universe. Life is not always fair, people will often disappoint us, and we cannot control the external world. Things don't always go according to plan. It will make life that much easier and enjoyable if we accept these facts of life.

42

Are you looking for what's wrong or what's right?

The answer to this question will determine how you feel and your outlook on life. Your outlook on life will be reflected in how you experience life, because our attitudes not only determine how we think, but they also actually determine our reality!

Are you always looking at what is wrong, what doesn't work, and how bad things are? Consider how that makes you feel and what it does to your general perspective.

Are you looking at everything that is wrong about your divorce, or have you considered what might be right about it?

Or, are you looking at what you do possess and the opportunities and possibilities that are before you now? Are you looking at everything your ex did wrong, or are you giving him or her some credit for what they might have done right?

Ask yourself: Am I looking at what is right or what is wrong?

43

Understand your limited perspective.

When you are in pain, you have a very limited perspective. It is like being in a dense fog. Even in the fog, there is still a great deal happening and available out there. You just cannot see it through the limited perspective of the fog. The same goes for divorce.

When we are in pain and confusion, our ability to see the big picture is severely restricted. Our pain and sadness color everything we see and do. We are not perceiving clearly.

As time passes and you begin to heal, you will once again begin to experience life in a more positive light, and the world will begin to open up for you once more. You will begin to see opportunities, hidden gifts, life lessons, new possibilities, and a new life.

Remember, this time of pain will pass. Things will get better.

44

Regain your power, and take full responsibility.

A victim places blame on someone else or something other than themselves. By doing so, they absolve themselves of responsibility for their life and their feelings. As a result, they give away all their power and the ability to control their own life.

By blaming someone else, you are essentially saying that you are not responsible—and that the person you blame is. If they hold your life in their hands, then they have enormous power over you: You have given them control and abdicated your own power.

By taking full responsibility for your part in your divorce and marriage, as well as for your present life and how you feel, you take back control and power. You can now be the sole mistress or master of the ship of your life.

Blame keeps you stuck in the pain and renders you inept. Responsibility gives you back your life.

45

There is a cost in being right.

Some of us are willing to give up our happiness and well-being just to be right. The costs of being right are high. In a divorce, it is all too often about being right—which leads to great self-righteousness, indignation, and misery.

Being right is a function of a wounded ego. It is amazing the price that people are willing to pay just to be right: their peace of mind, health, happiness—You name it! Why do you have to be right? What are you trying to prove? Who are you intent on making wrong and why? What will it accomplish in the long run? Is it really worth it?

Sometimes it's better to give up the suffering involved with being right and simply move forward in your life. Being right may give you some instant gratification but it gets you nowhere in the long run.

Let it go. Let it be.

46

Consider that things just might happen for a reason.

What if this divorce just might be happening for a good reason? Could it be possible? Might there a bigger plan out there for you, a better future that you can't see right now? Are things occurring so that you might evolve into the person you are meant to be?

Sometimes you have to give up the life you have for the life you are meant to live. Sometimes you have to give up who you were to become who you are meant to be.

What if there is a brighter future awaiting you? What if this is happening for your benefit? What if there are incredible possibilities and opportunities awaiting you in your new life? What if your divorce is the catalyst for an incredible new life?

What if?

47

Don't make decisions based on feelings.

O ur feelings change from day to day . . . sometimes from hour to hour. They are just feelings and as such are transient. Don't judge them or act on them, because you may very well feel totally different in the morning.

Say you are angry at your ex and you call your attorney and instruct him to do something that makes no sense at all and ends up harming you? That's what I'm talking about.

Wait it out. See what happens and see how you feel in 24 hours. Don't make decisions based on feelings.

48
Make choices from your higher self.

When you are faced with making a choice, and we make hundreds of them every day, choose from that place within you that knows what is just, moral, and true. Don't allow the wounded ego that simply reacts in a negative fashion to determine the course of your life.

Your higher self, that place where your inner wisdom resides, is the place where you will make choices that will always result in your highest interest being served.

Be that higher self that resides within each of us.

49
Don't expect help from your ex

After nearly 20 years of marriage, my habits as they pertained to my ex were pretty fixed. I continued to call him when I needed help with the kids and became upset when he didn't drop what he was doing to come to my aid. I expected him to be emotionally supportive and there for me. Wrong.

It took my marriage counselor to wake me up and remind me that I was barking up the wrong tree. My husband was no longer my husband and all the things that I expected of him were unrealistic.

Don't go to your ex for help and moral support. Start counting on other people. Build a support network. Your spouse no longer has that job.

50
Distinguish between what you can and cannot control in life.

So much of our suffering and unhappiness comes from trying to control the uncontrollable. Here it is in a nutshell: The only thing you can control in life is you and your reactions to life. Period.

We cannot control the external world or the people in it. If you examine the course of your life, you will see that this theory has been proven to be true over and over. Were you ever able to control your ex? Were you ever able to control what life brought your way?

Knowing the difference between what you can and cannot control will free you. We cannot control what happens, but we can control how we handle what happens.

51
Get rid of anger in healthy ways.

*E*xtreme anger is a killer. Anger has one target: You.
Learn to get rid of anger in healthy ways: Exercise at a brisk pace to burn it off, get a plastic bat and beat the hell out of your pillows, scream in the woods, or channel the energy generated by anger to accomplish something that needs doing.

Process your anger: Examine it, and determine what is underneath it. A good amount of the time we find that anger is a cover for sadness.

If you don't handle your anger in healthy ways, it will turn on you.

52
Stop reactive behavior in its tracks.

*O*ur emotions can take over and cause severe damage in our lives. The right side of the brain that controls emotions reacts much faster than the rational left side. Sometimes emotions are so quick to explode that we don't realize we are overreacting until we are in the midst of or over a blowup.

Get conscious and pay attention to the cues your body sends you such as tensed muscles or a fluttering heart rate. When you notice that you are heading into your danger zone, that place where your emotions will take over and cause you to say and do things you will regret, do the following:

Stop! Excuse yourself and walk away from whatever is

causing the upset. Go to a quiet place and sit down and do about three minutes of deep breathing, focusing only on the physical sensations of your breath. Then visualize something or someone that brings you a deep sense of peace or joy. Connect to that feeling. Sit with that for a minute or two. Then think about how you want to handle the stressful situation.

Take the time- out and center yourself. Don't let your emotions and reactive behavior run the show.

53
Don't take it personally.

All too often we take the things our ex did or is presently doing too personally. Then we feel terrible about ourselves and create disempowering meanings about ourselves.

If your ex had an affair and lied, you feel betrayed and make it all about you. You might think: I must not have been good enough or I was unlovable. That's taking it personally.

Turn it around: Instead of taking it personally, look for the impersonal. Perhaps your ex doesn't have moral boundaries.

Always look for the impersonal aspect. Your ex probably didn't enter your marriage with the intention of having an affair—It happened. It might be more about them and less about you.

Take this principle and apply it to your life in general. We simply take too many things personally and cause unnecessary upset and hurt. More often than not, it is not about you. You would be surprised how not about you it is.

Always look for the impersonal aspect.

54
Everyone sees things differently.

*L*ife is a largely a matter of interpretation, and each of us interprets things differently according to who we are, our emotional baggage, and our perspective on life.

Your divorce story is probably very different from your ex's version, all filtered through each of your different personal experiences. Usually there is your story, their story, and the truth is somewhere in between.

Remember the inkblot test? An inkblot is presented to a patient and they are asked what they see. One person sees a butterfly, yet another sees a storm cloud. Who is right? Neither. Who is wrong? Neither.

Don't expect your ex to understand, know, or do things as you would—You are two different human beings. We all see things through our own set of eyes.

55
Help yourself during your divorce.

Stress, anxiety, anger, and all the other negative emotions of divorce break you down physically and mentally. A continual rise in the production of the stress hormone cortisol causes big-time damage. It harms the functioning of your immune system, clouds your thinking, raises your blood pressure, strains your heart—Get the idea?

During your divorce and even afterward, it is mandatory that you do whatever you can to combat the effects of stress. Exercise to burn off stress and anxiety, get proper rest (sleep deprivation has its own set of negative effects), eat well, do calming exercises such as yoga or meditation, and pamper and nurture yourself.

If you want to be able to handle your divorce and life after your divorce, give yourself a helping hand.

56
What emotional baggage did you bring to your marriage?

*E*ach of us brings some sort of emotional baggage from our past into our marriage. Perhaps you were overly sensitive, an enabler, a worrier, too bossy, insecure, overbearing, had low self-worth, or were too demanding. Now is the time to address those issues that do not serve you, the same ones that did not serve your marriage.

Clean it up so it doesn't get in the way of your future. Recognize the baggage and where it came from, and then realize that for the most part your emotional baggage is probably a meaning you created about yourself from something in your past.

For instance: Your parents were highly negative and so as a child you decided that you were not good enough. You turned that into a subconscious core belief about yourself and have lived your life according to that belief. The truth is that your parents were negative. Period. You attached to that fact the meaning that you weren't good enough, but it is only a meaning that you created and not a fact! Yet you carried that into your marriage and then allowed your ex to bully you because you didn't feel good enough—Get it?

Use this divorce as a catalyst to heal all the emotional baggage you have been carrying around for years, and become free to be who you were meant to be!

57
What is the true nature of life?

Have you accepted the true nature of life?

The nature of life: Life is not always fair nor is it a bowl of cherries. Life is unpredictable, ever-changing, filled with opposites, i.e. good and bad, joy and sorrow, easy and hard, up and down, etc. Life offers no guarantees. That's life, and your divorce is just a microcosm of life.

Get real, and accept the facts of life. Don't expect life to be anything other than it is.

58
It's all about choice.

The most valuable and powerful trait of our humanity is our free will and the ability to choose for ourselves.

We get to choose how to live our lives and how to handle what life throws at us. We can choose to live as a victim or as a responsible person. We get to choose to see possibilities or impossibilities in life. We can choose to be bitter or accepting, happy or sad, willing or unwilling . . . .

We can choose to forgive and to be free of the past or to live with resentment and unhappiness for the rest of our lives.

It's all a matter of choice, and you are the one who gets to choose.

59
Consider the costs.

*I*f you cannot let go of blame, resentment, regret, bitterness, or anger, ask yourself this question: What is it costing me to hold on?

Is holding on to negative attitudes costing you your precious time? Your peace of mind? Your health? Your well-being? Your children's well being? Your future? Trust me, it isn't hurting your ex one iota. You bear the full brunt of holding on.

Letting go is a gift you give yourself. Letting go allows you to be free of your past and to be totally present in the here and now and to do what you need to do to create a new and fulfilling life.

60
What forgiveness is not.

Forgiveness is the final frontier in divorce recovery. You may be highly resistant to the idea of forgiveness because you think you are letting someone off the hook or saying what he or she did was acceptable. Not so.

Forgiveness is not condoning bad behavior or forgetting. It is not about reconciliation or being friends. It is not about absolution. You decide what forgiveness is for you.

Forgiveness is about giving yourself the gift of freedom from all the negative emotions that are dragging you down and keeping you stuck. It's recognizing that as human beings we all have our stuff, our emotional baggage, and we all do things we might later regret. It's about the wounded child within each of us and the compassion that we can muster for that wounded child.

Forgiveness will set you totally free to create a wonderful life after divorce. Both forgiveness of self and others does that. It releases all the obstacles that stand in your way to that life. It is truly the ultimate gift you can give to yourself.

61

Create a vision of your future, and be it now.

*C*reate your future self by visualizing it. Visualize yourself a year or two down the road. Who do you want to be and what do you want to be doing?

See the person you aspire to become, and start being that person now! Act the part of the person you picture because what you are being is what you will become.

Why wait? Even if you have to fake it, just do it. If you want to be more loving, be more loving now. If you want to be more self-sufficient, start acting like a self-sufficient person acts.

Be your future now.

62

Use this divorce as a catalyst for personal growth.

This divorce can serve as the crisis or the epiphany you need to wake you up and begin to make the changes you have always meant to make in your life. That's what it usually takes for dramatic change in your life: a dramatic, eye-opening experience.

Your divorce has many life lessons and deep wisdom to impart to you if you are willing to listen. Use your divorce as a way to facilitate personal growth. Take the lessons and grow as a human being. Evolve into the person you were meant to be.

All too often, people go through tough times and don't make the effort to glean the wisdom and growth from that experience. What a waste! Don't waste the opportunity for forward movement.

63

Where are you placing your attention?

How you are feeling and how you are functioning can be reflected in where you are placing your attention.

Is your attention on what is wrong or right in your life? Is it on what you don't have or what you do have? Is your attention placed on the little things on your to-do list or on the big issues before you? Is your attention placed on everything you can do to let go and move forward? Where is your attention?

Examine where your attention is these days, because where it is will reflect where you are going.

64

Transformation is a lifelong pursuit.

*T*ransformation doesn't happen once and then last forever. You may have an epiphany, but it won't remain with you without your commitment and effort—for the rest of your life. Sorry, but that's just the way it is.

Personal growth, happiness, and fulfillment are lifelong pursuits. The more you know the more you realize you don't know. Just like a runner who stops training, we cannot expect to live a transformed without putting in that constant effort and commitment to ourselves.

The effort you put in is what you will get out.

65

We do the best we can with the resources at hand.

Zen motto on Hospice door: "We will do what we can now with mindfulness and compassion, and when we can do more we will."

When we were children, we did what we could with the knowledge that we had at that particular point in time. It is no different now.

In terms of your divorce, you did the best you could with the resources you had at the time. The good part is that you now have more resources: knowledge, experience, and invaluable life lessons that will allow you to grow and hopefully not repeat those things that did not serve you.

66
Take the objective stance.

When the going gets tough, remove yourself from the stressful situation at hand, take a few deep breaths, and assume an objective stance.

Take yourself out of the equation and be a third party observing the action. This will give you the ability to see the bigger picture and see the positions of both individuals involved.

Pretend you are the coach, and see how differently things look from that perspective. Being objective and removing yourself from the emotional aspect of the situation will allow you make choices you never imagined.

67
Reduce
significance.

Handle a stressful situation by reducing its significance. Again, take a look at the bigger picture.

As already mentioned, when you are in upset, step back and take a time out. Ask yourself: Is it a matter of life or death? Will this be such a big deal a year down the road? Is it really worth the misery? Are your emotions turning it into something bigger than it really is? What are the costs to you?

We tend to make mountains out of molehills. Don't.

68
Your marriage and your divorce were co-creations.

No one person is ever to blame or to be held 100% responsible for the end of a marriage. Your marriage and your divorce are co-creations of both people involved. Remember, there are two people in every relationship.

Even if you were in an abusive relationship, you allowed it. Taking responsibility for your part will grant you many gifts: power, ways to grow, an abdication of blame and resentment, and the resulting freedom from the past and its pain.

69
Stop judging yourself.

*I*f you are feeling low, having negative thoughts, or experiencing upsetting feelings, try not to judge yourself too harshly. Show yourself the same love and compassion you would offer a child or a friend.

Feelings and emotions are transitory, they change all the time. Don't judge your feelings. They are simply feelings.

Judging yourself only makes you feel worse. Start to notice how often you are placing judgment on what you do and say.

Judging only creates more mind chatter and low self-esteem. Nobody judges you as harshly as you do yourself. Try being a bit more gentle with yourself.

70

Your divorce is not just a simple life change: It is a full-blown life transition.

*D*ivorce and separation are only less severe than the death of a loved one in terms of life losses. It is not just a change; it is a life transition, something marked by very specific phases.

A life transition is a time in life when the entire fabric of your life is upended. Your very identity and the roles you held come crashing down.

A life transition is marked by both the grieving process and its attendant emotions as well as by a feeling of being in total limbo. Limbo is often referred to as a neutral zone, where you simply have no idea who you are and where your life is going.

Understand that you need time and nurturing. A life transition begins with an ending, followed by the neutral zone, and then moves to a new beginning. You need to be in that neutral zone for a while in order to move forward later. Go easy on yourself. Take the time for deep reflection and support.

Once you have gone through that period of limbo, you will move into acceptance, which completes the ending and gives you closure. From there you are free to create a new beginning.

71
The now is all that exists.

*T*he past is gone, never to return. It cannot be undone, and ruminating about what was doesn't alter it. There is no going back.

The future does not exist yet, and no one can predict it. All there is is the now.

The now is where you need to live. The now is where you will find acceptance. Letting go happens in the now.

72
Original intentions

Stuff happens in life. Change is the constant. Think back: What were your original intentions toward your ex when you first met? What were their original intentions toward you?

Did you intend to get divorced? To have an affair? To fall out of love? Doubtful.

Were your intentions back then to love and support each other? To get married, raise a family, and live happily ever after? Probably.

Life does not always work out as we originally intended, and painfully we learn that over our lifetime. But consider your original intentions.

73
Resistance and surrender.

*I*f you are holding on to what your life was then, you are resisting what your life is now—reality. It's like resisting a tornado as it bears down upon you, thinking that you can somehow make it stop. Acknowledging the tornado gives you the option of deciding how best to handle the situation.

What kind of energy does it take to resist? How does it make you feel? Does it change your present reality?

Resisting reality is an exercise in futility. Try surrendering to what is. Surrender is not giving up; it is accepting what is and going with the direction of your life. Once you can surrender to what is, you can then make realistic and powerful choices for your new life.

74
Our choices define us.

Your choices define who you are. We make thousands of choices during the course of our lifetime, and each carries a consequence, so make certain that you choose wisely.

Do so by asking yourself: Will this choice empower me or disempower me? Will it serve me or harm me? Is this choice about instant gratification or about achieving a long-term goal? Will this choice honor me or disrespect me? Will it move me forward or keep me stuck?

Think before you choose or make a decision, because every choice will ultimately define who you are and what your life will look like in the future.

75

Go to your heart's intelligence.

*H*eart Intelligence will prove to be your saving grace. You can think something to death. You go back and forth and back and forth.

Your head is the place where your wounded ego operates, and a wounded ego will dictate resistance, reactive behavior, righteous positions, and resentment.

Get out of your head and into your heart where your higher self resides. Your heart is where you will be able to bypass that wounded ego and access the intelligence of your heart. Your heart is the place to go to for unconditional love, compassion, empathy, courage, and forgiveness.

If you believe in karma, the theory that we will ultimately get back what we give, then you believe in the power of the intelligence of your heart to bring back to you what you give out.

There are good reasons that over the centuries the heart has been the subject matter of philosophers, writers, poets, composers, and sages.

76

Honor and understand the grieving process and the crazy times.

When you first separate or divorce, you fall head first into the grieving process. Any major loss in life is accompanied by this period of time where you are in denial, anger, sadness, depression, confusion, and fear.

Your emotions will be all over the place, and you will bounce back and forth among all these feelings. It is extremely painful, bewildering, and overwhelming, but it is part of the process of this life transition, and you must approach it as such.

You will go through crazy times where you can't believe the things you say and do. You will be angry and sad and confused.

This, too, shall pass.

77

You must create space for happiness.

Visualize a pie cut into pieces. Each piece represents an area in your life and what is happening there. Each slice takes up a portion of your time.

Now visualize how many slices are being taken up with worry, resentment, holding on, resistance, etc. If you want to access the opportunities and possibilities that are opening up for you, then you need to make room for them.

You have to make room for your future by letting go of the past. You need to make room for new activities, new thoughts, and new dreams. There is only so much room, and something's got to give.

78

The rock story: Let it go before you drown!

A woman is swimming across a lake holding on to a large rock. Needless to say it is weighing her down, and before long she starts to struggle. The people on the shore notice what is happening and call out to her to let go of the rock.

Yet she continues to hold on to the rock while attempting to cross the lake. One can see that she is tiring and struggling, and so the people on shore call out again: "Let it go!"

She doesn't, and now she begins to bob in and out of the water, gasping for breath! The people frantically call out to her to let go of the rock, and as she sinks below the surface of the water, they hear her cry out: "I can't, it's mine!"

What price are you willing to pay to hold on to your stuff?

79

Acknowledge that you may have ignored signs all along the way.

So often I hear from a client that they had no idea their marriage was about to implode. They claim it came as a total surprise. Yet upon further questioning and when willing to admit to the truth, they can see that there were warning signs all along.

I submit to you that there were indeed signs all along the way, maybe as far back as when you married! We choose not to see the signs, we deny them, or we see them but do nothing about those warning signs.

Once you allow yourself to see the truth of your divorce, you will see the signs along the way that led to the end of your marriage. What is most important now is to recognize what the signs meant and to ensure that they don't pop up in your next relationship or in your life in general, or that you recognize them early.

Life always gives us warning signs.

80
Try a new spin on things.

*I*f you have to constantly be attaching meaning to things, try interpreting them to your advantage, with a new spin.

For instance: You interpret the end of your marriage as you being a failure. How about the end of your marriage meaning that your marriage was not meant to be and that now you have finally been given the opportunity to do all the things that you never could do when you were married?

A *spin* is defined in the world of public relations as an interpretation of an event to persuade public opinion in favor of a certain organization or person. Try putting a positive spin on your divorce.

81
Cut the ties
that bind.

After all these years with your ex, you still have a strong, emotional tie between the two of you. Every time you engage with your ex, that tie can be activated, triggered, and strengthened.

If you want to let go and move on, then you need to cut that emotional cord between the two of you. You cannot have both the cord and the freedom.

Think of it this way: For an alcoholic to recover, they certainly wouldn't choose to hang out in bars, would they? Start the process of severing the ties that bind by keeping your physical and mental distance.

Concentrate on your recovery efforts without backsliding due to emotional triggers.

82
Who can you change?

Ask yourself if you have ever been able to successfully change another person? People have to want to make changes in their lives, and, no matter what you do, if they see no need to make positive changes it won't happen. Change comes from within.

If you look back over your life, you will undoubtedly find that attempting to change someone else has usually met with failure. Like trying to control what you cannot control in nature or society, trying to change a person is a futile endeavor.

Think about the changes you are now seeking. It took your full commitment and desire to change to make it work. No one else could have done that for you.

Don't delude yourself into thinking that you are finally going to change your ex. Now is the time for your own personal growth.

83

Your ex is no longer your business.

For so long, what our ex said and did was our business.

It takes time to realize that now they are no longer our business.

Where they go, what they do, who they hang out with, who they might be dating—All are not our concern anymore.

As long as support and custody agreements are being met, your ex-partner is simply not your business. To act as if they are still your spouse is a habit you are going to need to break.

84
Reconnect with your passions.

When you begin to consider what you want to do and who you want to be in your new life after divorce, it is important that you reconnect with your passions.

Your passions are the things that you love to do, the things that make you come alive, the things that bring you joy, and the things that resonate for you. Perhaps you love the act of creating, or giving back to society, or international travel and adventure, or horseback riding. Connect with your passions.

To reconnect to your passions, take a piece of paper and pencil and just let it flow out of you. Write down what you are passionate about, and when you have finished with your list go through the process below to come up with your top five passions. Just compare each one against the next and choose one over the other and then move on down the list.

So, for example, if you have ten passions, look at the first two and if you had to choose one over the other, which would it be? Then take that choice and compare it to the third item on the list. Do this until you get to the bottom of the list—The passion that has survived is your number one passion.

Go back and do the process all over again with the remaining items. Do this until you have your top five, and then begin to think of how you can incorporate these passions into your life, whether it is in your work or personal life.

Live your passions, and you will be happy. Wouldn't it be great to want to get up in the morning? Make certain the things you are most passionate about show up in your life.

85
Take small, actionable steps.

*T*he act of moving forward in life is best achieved through small, actionable steps.

Let me give you an example: Say you want to start exercising with the goal of getting in shape. Don't set yourself up for failure by jumping into this project full tilt. The surefire way to fail is if you take on far too much too soon. Temper your expectations.

Start out by establishing a schedule that is achievable given what you have been doing. Perhaps commit to three days a week of 20-minute walks. If you can accomplish that step, then you have empowered yourself to add additional challenges the next week.

Small achievable steps are the way to success in anything that you choose to take on. Recovery from a divorce is done in small, achievable steps so that each small step moves you on to the next one.

Use the SMART acronym: specific, measurable, achievable, realistic, and timely.

In coaching, we make certain our clients are in action every week. Being in action takes the place of ruminating about your pain. Stay in action.

86
Work backward toward your new goals.

Goal setting is best achieved by working backward. Your first step is to decide upon a goal and to describe it in detail. Once you have the vision of that goal, consider how long it will take you to achieve it. Make certain that you are being realistic.

Now work backward: Say you want to write a book and you want it completed in one year. Where would you have to be in six months if you are to reach your timeline goal? Once you know where you have to be in six months, determine where you need to be in three months? One month? This week?

Via this method, you can crystallize your action steps on a weekly basis and keep yourself on track. It works.

87
What do you value? Make certain it shows up in your life.

Your life after divorce is yours to create. There is a good possibility that who you were being in your marriage may not have been connected to what is important to you. Now is the time to reconnect.

Much like your passions, your values will move you forward into a fulfilling life. Say that you find that you truly value integrity but it has been absent for some time. Start having integrity show up in your life on a daily basis.

Think about what you value in life, and make certain you are being and living those values. I promise that you will soon find that you like yourself a great deal.

Not only that, your values showing up in your life will alter the very landscape of your life.

88

Create peace in the family for the kids.

*I*t is an ugly sight when two divorced people cannot manage to get along and therefore bring their tension into the family, i.e. their kids. It isn't so much the actual divorce that harms the kids but how you and your ex choose to be with each other during and after the divorce.

We all make sacrifices for our children, and now is the time for you to realize that for the kids to heal and be okay they need a supportive and nurturing environment, which does include two feuding parents.

Even if your ex is being uncooperative, you must do whatever it takes to protect your kids. Remember our children model themselves after us. How you are being is what is most important for them.

89
Watch out for friends' advice.

Our friends are well-meaning, loyal, and supportive—
usually. When we first separate, we love to tell our
divorce story in all its gory details, and our friends are there to
agree with us—especially when it comes to blaming our ex.

Initially there is nothing wrong with that, BUT more often than
not our friend's over-protectiveness gets in the way of the fact
that we must move on to face the truth about our situation and
assume responsibility if we are to heal.

I know a woman who felt she needed to establish boundaries
with her ex in order to keep herself emotionally safe, but her
friends wanted her to stand up to him (a bully) and let him have
it. Bad advice. She knew the best way to handle her ex, and she

also knew the price she would have to pay by pushing him into his danger zone of reactive behavior.

Be careful of your friends' advice. Listen to others, but trust your own instincts and inner wisdom.

90

Do the things you want to do before it is too late.

*L*ife is short, and it is up to you and you alone to make it sweet. If there are things that you want to do, do them now. When I was married my ex didn't care for snorkeling or scuba diving, and I loved them both. I loved sailboats, and he got sick on them. After my divorce, I got certified in scuba diving and went on to find a group of divers via the website meetup.com. Since then I have taken three incredible diving trips and plan on doing more.

Even if money is a concern, there is plenty you can do now that you couldn't or wouldn't do before. You are free to write your own itinerary, so do it.

91
Expand your horizons.

Get out there and do new things. Meet new people. Expand your horizons and raise the bar. Step outside the lines of the box you may have painted yourself into!

Being single again means you need new friends with whom to hang out. You will find that your married friends are just that: married. Don't take it personally when you aren't invited out any more on a Saturday night to couple outings.

You want to be with people who have similar interests now that yours have changed. Join clubs or organizations where you can make new friends.

Do new things. Join an art appreciation club. Take a continuing education course on literature. Visit museums you have not been to in ages. Take up kayaking. Get out there and partake of life.

92

Heal before you get involved in another serious relationship.

Rebound relationships can be very dangerous to your healing process. I always suggest that before you get into another serious relationship make certain that you have fully healed and moved on from the last one. Make certain that you have taken the life lessons from your divorce to heart so that you do not repeat anything that might harm you.

It is easy to get involved quickly and to place your well-being in another person's hands. Don't do it. If you have learned nothing from this divorce, at the least learn that you and you alone are responsible for your well-being, self-esteem, and ultimate happiness. Don't place them in another's hands.

Look at dating initially as a way to meet new people, have new experiences, and get back into life.

93

Honor and respect yourself, or no one else will.

Self-esteem and confidence will return once you have let go and moved on. You must always give yourself credit for all you have accomplished and endured. It goes beyond simply being your own champion. You must deeply honor and respect yourself.

You deserve that honor and respect. In every choice you make, consider yourself. Be your greatest advocate. Be your best friend. Be your biggest fan.

Respect yourself in all that you do. Unless you can give yourself that respect, others will not.

You are a one in a million, a totally unique human being who will not pass this way again.

94
Memorize the serenity prayer.

*T*his incredible prayer is something you should tape to your medicine cabinet and read every single day! I have put in parentheses some substitutions if the religious feel does not work for you.

Also, consider that the word *change* can be interchanged with the word *control*.

From Reinhold Niebuhr:

God grant me the serenity
to accept the things I cannot change;
courage to change the things I can;
and wisdom to know the difference.

Living one day at a time;
Enjoying one moment at a time;
Accepting hardships as the pathway to peace;
Taking this world
as it is, not as I would have it;
Trusting that He (Life) will make all things right
if I surrender to His (Life's) Will.
Amen.

95
Welcome the future.

A famous author described the transformation of her father starting at the age of 65 when he retired from his official job. He began to read, something he had never done. He took the bus to a university 30 miles away and enrolled in classes in areas that fascinated him. He started to travel, this man who had never been more than 50 miles from home. He transformed himself and his entire life. It bore almost no resemblance to the one he had lived for the previous 65 years. He blossomed.

You can do the same. This does not have to be the end of your life. It can be the beginning of a new life. There is so much out there ready for you to take. Consider this older man's story and realize that if you so desire, life can begin anew.

About the author

SHELLEY STILE is a professionally trained and certified Divorce Recovery Life Coach. She works with individuals undergoing divorce or who have recently divorced, guiding them through the process of letting go, moving on, and creating a new life afterward. Shelley works to allow her clients let go of the pain of the past and all its attendant negative emotions as well as to be in full acceptance of what life is now: acceptance without blame, resentment, or regret.

Shelley trained with the prestigious Coaches Training Institute. She did additional training in divorce recovery with the Ford Institute for Integrative Coaching's Spiritual Divorce. She is a certified Life Coach (ACC) via the International Coaches Federation, the governing body of the worldwide Life Coaching industry.

Shelley has taught classes at the Adult Schools of Montclair and Chatham, New Jersey, as well as leading workshops at the professional Women's Center in Montclair, New Jersey, and the Center for Women in Livingston, New Jersey.

Shelley herself underwent a divorce, so she knows firsthand the journey that must be made in order to recover and thrive afterward. Having been there, she has the gift of being able to fully empathize with her clients.

Shelley coaches her clients via telephone, so you can be anywhere and be coached.

Visit her website at www.lifeafteryourdivorce.com and receive her free ebook on coping with divorce at www.freedivorcesupportbook.com and receive her free monthly newsletter Take Back Your Life After Divorce.

Made in the USA
San Bernardino, CA
13 August 2013